ILLUMINATIONS

ILLUMINATIONS

Musa Muhaiyaddeen

THE WITNESS WITHIN, LLC.

Cover painting by Amy Wilson

For more information about her paintings and calligraphy, please
contact her at: **aw786@yahoo.com**

Library of Congress Control Number: 2018903627

Muhaiyaddeen, Musa

    Sufi Illuminations / Musa Muhaiyaddeen
    Atlantic City, NJ: The Witness Within, Inc., 2013
    p. cm.

    Trade paperback: 978-0-9965655-6-1
    Also available in Kindle, Epub and iPad formats.

    1. Sufism. 2. God. 3. Truth. 4. Wisdom. 5. Reality. 6.
    Enlightenment. 7. Eternal Life. 8. Transformation. I.
    Title

Printed in the United States of America
First Printing

This book is dedicated to my teacher,
Muhammad Raheem Bawa Muhaiyaddeen,
my wife Asiya, and my parents.

I have deep gratitude for everyone in my life, for
those who have assisted me, inspired me, and en-
couraged me to continue sharing the wisdom that
my teacher has guided me towards.

I would like to especially thank
Amy Wilson, Lawrence Didona, and Fatima Meyers.

Contents

Introduction by Musa Muhaiyaddeen

Sufism is one of the paths that explains and guides us towards our inner spiritual being, to that part of us that is beyond the senses. It brings us to a place where there is the possibility of experiencing an entirely different way of existence. This is an inner journey that opens our hearts to the treasures found within the qualities of God.

Through the teachings of Sufism we learn that to do this we need to change our focus from an elemental being to a spiritual being. We learn that this is done by changing our nature and attitude towards everything in our lives. The rules of the animal kingdom are that the strong survive and the weak do not survive. The Sufi path teaches us that there is a place that is not part of the animalistic nature we are born with. There is another place that comes from the Eternal where the qualities that exist there are kindness, love, mercy, compassion, truthfulness, and justice. These are the outpourings of love that created this world.

Love is the reason this world was created. Love is the answer to all of the questions that we have. Love is the understanding that sets us free, and separates us from our attachments to the hypnotisms and the magnetisms of our physical existence. Love is the pathway that brings us to God.

Sufism is the path of love. This book is made up of quotes that are intended to stimulate the opening of the heart. They are intended to create a resonance that breaks the shell that hides the truth. This resonance is connected to the eternal resonance of the Creator. These quotes are examples of a methodology for bringing the spiritual self into being.

I was fortunate enough to have had a spiritual teacher. The contemporary Sufi Shaikh Muhammad Raheem Bawa Muhaiyaddeen, who guided me personally for fourteen years in the way of the heart. He instructed me to take what he had taught and share it with others. This book of quotes is an effort to fulfill the request of my teacher to bring the resonance of God into the hearts of others. My intention is for us all to experience the truth of existence, to free ourselves from being bound to the illusory nature of the senses, and that we may learn that there exists within us a universe, more worthy of exploring than all of the elemental pleasures in the world.

May it come to pass that these words resonate to break the shell of illusion that covers our hearts. May these words help take us to the eternal place where truth exists, and where love and kindness exist as reality. May our path towards God be straight and true and easy. *Āmīn.*

PART

The Sufi path to unlock the mysteries of existence is the study of compassion, mercy, patience, contentment, and love.

We must become compassion, we must become mercy, we must become tolerance, kindness, and justice. As we become all this, the influence of the material world lessens, and we begin to vibrate with reality.

The potential to love unconditionally exists within us, and when it begins to flow it is endless.

If we form the intention to serve others and follow that path, the truth which is our birthright will be revealed to us.

True compassion comes from God. It can come through a purified person who then distributes it as His compassion.

As long as we are unaware that we have fallen, we find no reason to climb up. It does not take any effort to fall, to rise we must engage effort.

When true love and compassion exist within us we feel the pain of others, the hunger of others, we acquire the ability to feel what others feel.

Truth is already within us, reality is already within us. We need to discover this and let them come forth.

Understand what is temporary and what is eternal. There is an Eternal Power that runs through everything. Get to know this Power. We need to spend time with this Power.

To remember our Creator we need to yearn for Him as we yearn for water when we are desperately thirsty.

Sufism is a path of transformation, a path of genuine inner work. This inner work is not something to talk about, it is something to become.

⁂

We need to start over again each day, start over with the intention to be on God's path, allowing Him to guide us, accepting what happens.

⁂

Let us make each other joyful, let us help each other, rejoice in each other's success, and be grateful.

⁂

Those of us who are on a spiritual path need to bring love to the equation. We need to bring love to whoever is around us, bring love to every situation we are in.

⁂

If we are not in the moment, we are in the past or the future, not in reality.

We need to watch our inclinations, and determine which are appropriate and which are not.

The less important the world is to us, and the less our well-being is contingent on the world, the more transcendent we are capable of becoming.

We need to understand ourselves, study ourselves, and be one within ourselves. Intend to have the words which come from our mouths be straight, clean and pure, without self-motive, filled with love.

If we separate ourselves from obligation to each other we separate ourselves from obligation to God.

For generosity to come from a clear place, it cannot come from the mind. It needs to come spontaneously from where our soul resonates. It needs to come from where our heart resides.

On the path of truth, on the path towards understanding reality, we need to let go of everything that we know. We need to start over. There needs to be a rebirth away from our past.

We are all meant to be glorious. Do not be afraid to be glorious.

When we remove the need for reward we become more sincere, hypocrisy leaves us.

There are so many things in this world which will give rise to doubt, we need to be steadfast no matter the circumstances.

Sincerity means doing what is correct without any thought of reward or punishment, doing it only because it should be done.

We do not need intermediaries for a mystical experience.

Our lives are like a theatrical play we need to disengage from in order to find the place where we connect to the reality of existence.

We need to remove ourselves from conflict, not with cowardice but with bravery.

The difference between a state and a station is the difference between being somewhere for a fleeting moment and being in a place where we actually stay, we live there.

We need to rid ourselves of the preconceptions which limit what we see.

Only in a state of gratitude do we enter the bliss of true surrender.

❀

If we are not watching, we do not learn anything, the moments go by in reaction.

❀

If we cannot take compassion to the place where it is for everyone, where it is non-discriminatory, where it does not see differences among people, then we are reinterpreting God's compassion for our own needs, and for our own set of desires.

❀

We cannot be full of the world and expect simultaneously to be full of God.

❀

To understand the mystery of unity we need to let go of the ego.

9

We need to hold everything we hear up to the light of God.

※

Once we center the way we understand and look at things, center our attitudes, we can move into a state of being which knows peace and contentment. This is the only way to enter the doorway to reality.

※

What do we need to know in order to know our Lord, our God? We need to know ourselves. If we do not know ourselves, we cannot know others. If we do not know ourselves and others, we cannot know God.

※

If the state of our consciousness is love, love will guide us.

※

If we think a hateful, contemptuous, or angry reaction is appropriate in certain circumstances, understand that what we are is what we carry around with us.

Belief is not actuated until it becomes an integral part of the way we are, an integral part of the way we act.

Divine law exists to align us with the natural flow of things, the Divine flow.

Are we more beautiful arriving or departing, are people glad to see us, or relieved when we go? We need to try to understand who we are, and how and why others react to us. We need to study ourselves, do we love or abuse?

We need to examine everyone in our lives. Our lives may depend on this. The friends and associates that we deal with have a great influence on the nature of our existence. If we have inappropriate friends and associates, they will take us to inappropriate places.

Gratitude gives us an understanding of our relationship to the One who gives.

When we are too busy trying to center others, we cannot center ourselves.

※

Have patience, avoid haste, sit still long enough for repose, for peace. From peace comes love, from love comes peace, they are intertwined.

※

We have the capacity to establish the nature of our existence—it is determined by each act of our lives.

※

We are pulled into the past by our attachment to it, and we are pulled into the future by our imagination of it.

※

God is already within us, He is not a stranger, He created us, He blew breath into us, and placed our soul within us. We need wisdom to analyze and understand this.

If we are resentful, we will be resented. If we cannot empathize with others, others will not empathize with us. If we cannot love, we will not be loved.

Creation itself is always in a state of perfection. It is only our inability to stay within perfection that keeps us in a state of duality.

Let us search for a love which is not elemental, not magnetic, search instead for a love which bypasses the elements, allowing mercy and compassion.

We live simultaneously in the world of the visible and the world of the invisible. Our fate should not be sought in what we see, but in what we do not see.

Overreaction is one of the enemies we face. Learning to treat each situation with an appropriate response is an acquired technique.

As human beings our qualities and actions define us.

Our own consciousness is what creates our future.

As we become more integrated with wisdom, duality disappears and we become one. Here is the secret— the ultimate watcher is the Divine Presence. Our consciousness watches and assesses our actions and qualities as we strive to be integrated with the Divine Presence.

God exists, He is merciful, compassionate, and loving. We need to believe this profoundly, it needs to be the basis of our understanding, thoughts and beliefs.

Freedom comes when our relationship with the world becomes less important, and our relationship with God becomes more important.

Wisdom is the door to peace.

※

Observe the lives of the most exalted beings, see how they help those around them with their qualities, let us emulate them.

※

Desire buries our consciousness and wisdom. Everything disappears but the need to satisfy that desire.

※

When we lose our faith, doubt, fear, and anxiety creep in.

※

Every act of kindness is a prayer.

※

When we feel what others feel we understand their hunger as we understand our own.

When we are in an unloving state we cannot be aligned with God.

Our attitude and our qualities create our state.

If we go on this path of becoming what we were created to be, there should be no question that God will help us towards that goal. That is why it is said that if we take one step towards God, He will take ten steps towards us.

Love changes everything.

When empathy is sincere, wanting nothing in return, it can be the doorway to a state of sincerity with God.

In our relationships with each other we should be treating each other with the respect of knowing that God exists within each of us.

The teachings of the holy beings are like rain which falls everywhere. There is great joy for those who collect this rain.

❊

Every encounter with another one of God's creatures is a test of how we are doing.

❊

When we think we are in control we have lost sight of reality.

❊

Mysticism is the ability to bypass all the hypnotic fascinations of the world, it is the ability to be in touch with that part of ourselves attached to what created us, that which is beyond our temporary manifestation.

❊

The opportunity for prayer exists with every breath.

As we see the light of God's Divine Radiance in everything we look at, our perception changes, we see things differently.

If we want to change our destiny, if we want to change who we are, we need to change our consciousness.

Intention is a vibration connecting us to the open space of God's holiness, our intention needs to be aligned with His.

Opinions block the truth, they stop us from seeing the truth, we believe we already know the answer.

We can never know who we are, we can never know what goes on within if we are busy reacting to everything in the elemental world.

When we know we are dealing with an awesome Power we are inclined to be careful interacting with it. Understand that there is an awesome Power in each human being, the Power of God, the most awesome Power in existence.

The results of what we do is not in our hands, but the way we act is. We cannot determine results in this world, but we can act in a fashion that is acceptable to God.

No matter where we are, no matter who is with us, no matter the circumstances, we need to remember one thing, the Divine Presence is always here within us.

If being involved in worldly situations means losing our connection to God, let us make the connection to God our priority, let us not justify our worldly state. Make God's love important enough to cancel out all other states.

If we invite love into our being it has friends. Love's friends are mercy, tolerance, compassion, and forgiveness.

Arrogance insists on having its own way, believing in its own correctness and its right to control. When arrogance cannot control by merely issuing a command it becomes anger.

The way we act determines who and what we become in the next moment.

We need to cleanse our words, cleanse our thinking, our actions. We need to make our actions pure, make them actions which are without malice, without improper motive. Unless we can bring ourselves to that place which has no improper motive, we are not cleansed.

Focus on peace rather than conflict.

If we have motives and expectations when we offer love, it is not offered in the right way.

❦

As soon as we point a finger we have limited our ability to comprehend.

❦

We need to return to the loving, kind, understanding beings we are supposed to be.

❦

There are healers who can touch us and make us feel better, they do this because they are conduits for our Lord who can do anything.

❦

It is as difficult for the beggar to give up his penny as it is for the king to give up his kingdom. God asks the same thing of everyone. Everything.

Understand that our ability to love is what saves us.

✿

Once we get into the state of correct action, we can get into the state of correct being.

✿

Self-motive brings about separation.

✿

Truly great holy beings treat everyone the same way, with the same love, they have no sense of differences. This is mysticism, this is the heart of it.

✿

To become a perfected human being requires deliberate consciousness in every action.

✿

The Sufi path is about a state of becoming and a state of being.

To step into reality we need to step out of the world.

Since everything is ruled by love, we need to start considering how we conduct ourselves daily. We need to ask ourselves if love is in our every action, or if we have abandoned love because we believe what we are striving for is more important.

We live in the world and we must do so appropriately, with dignity, and respect. At the same time we need to find dignity and respect in our relationship with God.

God's qualities bring wisdom, wisdom brings Divine Light, Divine Light brings higher consciousness and alteration of who we are, from animal to human to Divine human being.

If these three things do not happen: recognizing our state, assessing our appropriateness, and trying to change ourselves, we are not on the path.

23

When we are no longer bound by prejudice, by systems of beliefs, but are bound instead by the influences of love, mercy, and compassion, everyone around us benefits.

What separates us from each other separates us from God.

Forgiveness is the alchemy changing the acid we carry around.

The results of what we do is not in our hands, but the way we act is.

When doubt enters, we lose faith in the mercy, compassion, and love of the Creator, we lose faith in Him.

Walk love around, hand it out, love is not something to keep for ourselves.

Understand how to walk appropriately, how to act appropriately, to be positive in our relationships with others, and bring forth our own potential by bringing out the potential in others.

❄

Darkness and illusion only need to start the conversation, once it has begun we are no longer focused on reality, we are focused on something else which we convince ourselves is appropriate.

❄

True love will not let us be resentful, will not let us be jealous or angry. True love is a fire burning these things away.

❄

If we look at our lives carefully we understand we have no true satisfaction until we begin to walk the path towards our Lord, yearning to become intimate with our Lord.

When anger comes into our being it invites all of its friends. The friends of anger are resentment, hatred, and jealousy.

❀

We need to stop rationalizing our conduct enough to understand that our connection to our Creator is through love, and this connection is more important than any worldly situation.

❀

Great saints and holy beings came as translators for reality, they came as examples of reality.

❀

If we are to change, we must do away with our arrogance and ignorance.

❀

The qualities of God that we imbibe and become are the core to our becoming a true human being.

Gratitude is a door opening our connection to God, it permits an understanding of Him we cannot have without it.

❀

The greatest gifts are to be able to develop true love for humanity, which God created, and true love for God.

❀

To come close to compassion and mercy something must happen inwardly, the heart must open.

❀

Inner change will only happen when we make an active effort to change.

❀

The ocean of illusion becomes still only when we dive very deep, our focus must be deep and powerful.

❀

We need to trust in God, have faith, and make a great effort.

Mysticism is the study of the great mystery, who we are, and why we are who we are.

God is merciful. We should be merciful.

We have no control over anything in the world, the only control we have is to choose God. Everything we look upon as our having control of is an illusion we have made into our reality.

Faith is greater than any treasure that we can get from the world. Faith overcomes all of our difficulties. Faith disolves despair. This is the strength of faith.

Mercy, contentment, and gratitude do not depend on what we have on the outside, they depend on who we are inside.

We need to understand the qualities which belong to God and those which belong to the world, then shift our focus to those which belong to God.

Understand the difference between important things and insignificant things. If we cannot endure small difficulties we will never be able to endure major difficulties.

If we truly have gratitude we are satisfied with our current situation. We can strive for change and still not be attached to the outcome.

Go where the unseen is, go to the place that is beyond our senses and beyond the solutions of the intellect, engage with the part of us that is the inner heart.

As we commit to change we must have patience and faith. We must use certitude and determination as the legs to walk this path or we will turn back.

The ability to know the difference between God's time and ours is part of being peaceful.

We must learn to see correctly. Nothing around us will change, what will change is our perception as we look at everything in a different way. The key is learning how to perceive, how to see, how to look.

We need to know what is in our hands and what is not. We need to have the peace to accept that certain things are out of our hands and in the hands of the One to whom the responsibility belongs.

Once we act appropriately in this world the door to the unseen world opens.

Insist upon love in our state of being, beg God for this.

We become more by helping others become more.

❀

We determine our dignity. Understand what this is. We should be known as someone who is reliable, whose word means something, whose presence is helpful.

❀

We need to go from the mind to the heart. We need to stop thinking and start feeling. This is the state of love that has no contingencies, the state of love that has no expectations, the state of love that loves for the sake of God, and loves for the sake of God's creations.

❀

Realize our lives are about intention, effort, and correct action.

❀

If our lives consist only of what we see, hear, and touch, what our sensory perceptions identify, nothing deeper than that, it is equivalent to looking at the surface of the ocean and saying that the surface is all there is to know.

We need to help ourselves grow spiritually and then help others grow spiritually.

As we become more centered in God's qualities we can help others.

To understand and embark on the path of the mystic we need to be very subtle. We need to be in touch with what makes us do what we do, understand the motives underlying our qualities determining our actions and our intentions.

If we understand God's intention and make that intention ours, then when the two merge, it is the time of miracles, the time when things happen which are beyond words and beyond description.

We can be a peacemaker when we are in a place of peace.

Act with sincerity for the sake of our Lord, not for a worldly reward.

❀

With God's qualities we can see the divinity in others.

❀

We need to learn that embracing others brings us closer to reality, that when we give of ourselves we receive so much more. Abundance comes from a place without end and there is always enough.

❀

First we should search for love within ourselves, then we will be able to see it in others.

❀

Our destiny changes as our consciousness changes.

❀

As long as we are reacting to the world we do not have time to respond to God.

Once we understand the difficulties of others, when their pain is the same as our pain, when their hunger is the same as our hunger, their joy is the same as our joy, then we have achieved freedom.

If we want to be true human beings we need to be transparent, without self-motive, without judgment, without the accepted behaviors of the world.

We need to find a balance so that we can live our lives in this world and simultaneously prepare for the next realm.

Enlightenment occurs outside our history and outside of time. It is the moment we break free of our existence in this world. We change worlds and pass through illusion into reality.

Without kindness we ruin ourselves and make life difficult for everyone else.

Submission in prayer is exalted. Understand the greatness of living in the world of inner contemplation and satisfaction, removed from the push and pull of the world around us.

We always find an excuse to impose our version of reality, and it is the insistence on our version of reality which keeps us from truth.

Everything changes when love is in the equation.

Our circumstances do not control us, our attitudes and our qualities do.

When we increase our effort, elevate our intentions, then we have raised our understanding of our purpose, then gratitude follows.

What we are given is in proportion to our ability to give and share, not in proportion to our ability to take. The more we give away the more we are given, the more we share our joy the more we are given.

In each moment either we are a believer or we are not, either we are conscious of God within us, in our lives, in our actions and in everything we do, or we are not.

If we do not have tolerance for others, if we do not allow others to go their own way, we have a good indication about ourselves, about our own position on tolerance.

As we remove our separations from others, our separations from God grow smaller and smaller and smaller.

It is said that Sufism is not a philosophy, it is a way of being. It is said that those who talk about it as a philosophy are not living it.

In our relationships we should contemplate whether we are looking to give or to take.

God's love is at the heart of everything.

One peaceful person can influence a population, imagine what fifty peaceful people can accomplish.

To be at peace is to be centered.

When we meet a difficulty with emotional distress it is an opportunity to examine the roots of our discomfort, an opportunity to look at ourselves in the moment.

If we do not recognize that becoming a perfected human being is within our possibility, we abandon our birthright.

Any act of kindness is the same no matter our religion, our color, our country, or our language. It is still kindness.

Recognize that we have constantly changing states, whatever state we are in at any given moment is the state controlling us.

That pause between recognizing a situation and taking action is the beginning of maturity.

Arrogance, the first quality of separation, initiates a chain reaction, acquiring other negative qualities to reinforce itself.

We need to correct our attitude so that the drama of the world is less important to us, and our ability to go to a place of silence is increased. When we are still, the vibration and resonance of truth can be felt and understood.

Prophets, wise holy beings, saints and friends of God have been sent to us, religions have been sent, they are all instruction manuals.

We should focus on establishing compassion within ourselves.

If we go through life building up regret, then regret is what we become.

We are meant to understand that the physical act of prayer, the outer ritual is not enough, what happens on the outside is not enough, something needs to happen on the inside. We need to declare our intention and pray for inner transformation.

We must be careful about choosing those we associate with because they influence us, our friends can elevate us, or take us to the depths of hell.

Love is always available, it always exists. If we cannot see love it is not because of something outside of ourselves, it is because we are not looking deeply within.

※

When we enter the quality of gratitude an inner change occurs which alters our perception.

※

Becoming God's qualities is the way towards Him.

※

Can we stop thinking of ourselves as this body and think of ourselves as someone that spreads unconditional love? Who are we? Can we be a vehicle for God's love? Can we shift the perception of ourselves away from worldly definitions?

※

The work of a true human being is to be a beacon of God's light. As we wash externally with water we need to keep washing inwardly with love. We need to love God, love ourselves, and love His creations.

If we cannot love, none of the prayers or the things we do can make us a true human being.

❦

Family, tribe, and nation do not have precedence over the rest of humanity, we share humanity with everyone.

❦

To be the quality of graciousness we need to be gracious, to be the quality of compassion we need to be compassionate, to be the quality of mercy we need to be merciful, to be the quality of justice we need to be just.

❦

Being a lover of God is not about ourselves, it is about our interaction with others, how we see them, how we approach them, how we treat them.

❦

Within us is a place which intuitively understands whether we are in balance or not, whether we are aligned with what is true or not.

Love has enormous influence and power, it can accomplish amazing things, yet we cannot weigh it, measure it, or quantify it.

Understand the difference between elemental love and God's love which is not attached to the world, not attached to illusion, this is where mercy and compassion exist.

Our faith is not firm without effort.

Our destiny that is intended for us is to become wise.

We need to empty ourselves when we go in search of truth.

When God's love exists within us, arrogance and the need for control do not exist.

Everything starts with an intention, the mind can set an intention, and words can set an intention. Our intention needs to come from the inner heart to guide us towards the reality of our existence.

The great holy beings teach us how to find our way back. We do this by changing our interests, becoming interested in God instead of the world. With every step we take we make a choice, do we choose God, or do we choose some interest in the world?

The steps taking us to wisdom are steps of appropriate inner thought, and appropriate outer action.

Opinions, thoughts, and emotions put blinders on us which limit our ability to see and to connect genuinely with others.

In our disappearing, God appears.

The truth is that our heart is our place of worship. Wherever we go we are always in a place of worship.

※

We are told that God loves our effort, this is our obligation. No one has said that God loves our expectations.

※

Our most exalted moments, our path to reality, is when we act with God's qualities, when we let them flow through us.

※

God has no favorites, God chooses the ones who choose Him. Then we become the chosen people. The treasure He has for us is the treasure of Himself which is beyond imagination.

※

Our serenity is a gateway to the entrance to reality. Our contentment is a gateway to the entrance to reality. We need to find that door. Be of the vibratory nature that can fit through that door.

Our intention may not bring about the results we want, but if our intention is correct we will be at peace with what is given that is appropriate for our state of being.

❁

To be still and do nothing in certain circumstances can be particularly hard work. We need to understand when action is necessary and when it is not, every situation requires this understanding.

❁

Gratitude does not allow for qualities such as hastiness, anger, resentment, or jealousy to reside within us.

❁

When our actions are God's actions we bring the experience of Divine Resonance to everyone around us.

❁

We need to set the right intention encompassed by love. When love fills a room there is no space for anything else.

Combine intention with breath. Breathe out the world of illusion, then inhale the reality of God.

Our intention creates our path, determining where we go. We need to look deeply into ourselves and analyze this.

Understand that what we do to others we also do to ourselves. If we want to save ourselves we must be careful not to harm anyone.

We are meant to be perfected, we are supposed to be saints.

God's qualities give us immunity to illusion, without them we are susceptible to the bacteria of illusion and the illnesses they cause: lack of respect, lack of empathy, hypocrisy, needing, grasping. These are all diseases of the heart.

Anything which is not one of God's qualities crowds out His qualities.

❀

We can make enormous change in others through the slightest tiny bit of kindness.

❀

The Sufi path is one of love, it is a path of unconditional love. We cannot form the right relationship with others unless we treat others with unconditional love. Unless we treat others in this way we cannot have proper respect for them, ourselves, or God.

❀

If we are incapable of recognizing those who are beyond us in wisdom, we are stuck in whatever state we are in.

❀

Everything is ruled by love. We are ruled by love, that is the point. This is not some outer exercise, we must strive to purify our inner state.

The eye of a hurricane is still, everything whirls around it. Every once in a while the hurricanes of our lives take hold of us, our circumstances catch us. It is just then that we need to find our still center space. That center is our protection, our sanctuary, the ability to avoid turmoil.

In the midst of chaos offer an axis of peace.

PART

TWO

We have a light body within us which is our reality, a connection we must be conscious of. This connection to God which resides within us exists on a level of consciousness, a level deep within the heart we need to be aware of. To be aware of it we need to engage specific qualities, qualities like gratitude. Gratitude is a door opening our connection to God, it permits an understanding of Him we cannot have without it.

Our lives are not about what we accumulate, our lives are not about the status we earn, not about the titles we receive, our lives are about the way in which we live. Our lives are about the qualities we have as we go through our existence. Our lives are about the qualities we have in our relationships, how much love and compassion we walk around with and carry with us from place to place.

There is a contemplative reality, a meditative realm, an unseen realm that we can be in touch with just as much as we can be in touch with the realm that we do see. When our physical needs that are constantly pushing and pulling us are not present we can find peacefulness in the unseen realm.

Understand the Sufi path and what it has to offer. Learn about this path by studying the examples of teaching masters who explain the uniqueness of unity, of being together as one, the uniqueness of what is present at the heart of this unity. When we resonate with that, we are in a peaceful state, there is nowhere else we need to be. We are at the center of the universe.

Everything which binds us to the world keeps us from reality, everything we consider important in the world keeps us from reality. We need to live in the world without expecting anything from it. Understand that there is reality and illusion, and know the difference.

The spiritual path is one of self-discovery. If our focus shifts from self-examination to what is going on with others, we have shifted from the spiritual path to something else, a path which is worldly, a path connected to motive, to power, the need to compare ourselves with others in order to feel that we stand up well in the comparison.

There is a maxim on this path that everything is ruled by love, a truth whether we accept it or not. Our own inner state determines whether or not we consider this to be true, it also determines how closely our own state is aligned with reality. The truth that everything is ruled by love is shorthand for what our lives should be like, what our attitude, our relationships, our inner state should be like. Once we understand this and see our own inner state with the light of this truth, we have a better idea of whether or not we are ruled by love.

We need to make the shift from our circumstances to God's qualities within ourselves. It is in this shift that we are going to find our freedom, it is in this that we are going to find the truth, it is in this that we are going to find our escape, it is in this that peace will be found.

Imagine what existence would be like if we were free of all of the things from our past and all of the things we imagine for our future. That freedom is available. We need to leave the past and let go of our expectations of the future. We need to understand reality is now.

People think they are in competition with everyone else. Their behavior and actions are based on this. To change this idea we need to look deeply within ourselves. Some people are too frightened to do this. We need to pass through this frightening stage. We may feel ashamed of what we have done, what we have experienced, ashamed of who we are, yet we must remember that we have a new opportunity to connect with God with every breath, that the universe is not only created by God, it is also sustained by Him, sustained with every breath, with constant new opportunities.

Doubt is a problem that causes so much turmoil. Doubt comes in different forms, it might surface through fear aroused by our expectations. When we have a list of expectations along with the accompanying fear that our plans will not turn out as we want them to, doubt creeps in. Doubt leads to misgivings. We begin to ask ourselves what we can do to create changes, what we can do to make things work out the right way. These expectations can lead to anxiety and exaggerated actions, even chaos as we attempt to control the outcomes in our lives.

If we look at the ocean from the sky or from a submarine we see two different aspects of the ocean, it is the same ocean but our perspective has changed. We need to submerge like a submarine, submerge within ourselves. This is a way to stop subjecting ourselves to all the irritations of the world, to stop subjecting ourselves to all the pushes and pulls of everything we come into contact with. If we are centered at our core we react from the inside, not in response to what is going on outside.

The truly great wise beings treat everyone the same way, with the same love, they have no sense of differences. This is mysticism, this is the heart of it. Mysticism is not about formulas, it is about the qualities we acquire, who we become. We know of the qualities of God: love, compassion, forgiveness, mercy, tolerance, to name a few. Why are they shown to us, why are they talked about? Why have we been given examples of these qualities in our lives? This is done to let us experience them so we can incorporate them into our own being.

When we establish conditions which encourage conflict, when we cannot love, we damage our capacity for reality, we damage our ability to make progress on the path towards God. Once we create situations in which we are inclined to be hateful, we have created a place within ourselves for hatred to exist. If we think a hateful or contemptuous reaction is appropriate in certain circumstances, understand that who and what we are in that moment is what we carry around with us. No matter where our anger is directed, no matter how righteous or appropriate we think that anger is, it is still anger, we have become vessels transporting anger, not love.

When we look at an ocean we see constant movement, even turbulence. Everything passing over the ocean affects its surface, but below, very deep, there is a stillness, different from what happens at the surface. Most people in the world are surface dwellers, but our consciousness functions beneath the surface of illusion. Accept that this space exists, dive deep into that place where the attachments and separations of the world leave us. We need to go to that space within ourselves while at the same time also live in the world.

We need to recognize that to make spiritual progress we must be centered. This means not having preconceptions, attitudes, or rigid assumptions determining the way things must be. Being centered means being free within the flow of what presents itself, taking what is given as it comes, using our wisdom and certitude with every situation.

Our Creator is compassionate, our Creator is merciful. God has given us the ability to experience compassion and mercy. When we taste this food of His, we come closer to Him. By coming closer to Him a new field of vision opens for us, new ways to see are opened, love which is our natural state begins to grow. With certitude we are moved with the knowledge that our Father is with us. We become stronger, more steadfast in certitude.

We need to live our lives in a way where everything we do can be on the front page of a newspaper. If we can do this and if we can be comfortable with this, our lives become easier because we do not have anything to hide.

As we purify ourselves we need to take our pure self to our Lord. Engage in a pure stream of conversation with Him, a pure stream of interaction with Him, a pure stream of knowing the reality that He is all that exists at this moment. In that we find contentment, in that we find peace, in that we find repose, we find the quiet, still place that is everlasting.

To step into reality we need to let go, we need to learn how to step away from the world, step out of the world. This cannot be something we play with, it must be what we do. We need to give up expecting anything from the world, give up wanting anything from it, and give up relying on it. We need to give up all our attachments to the world.

The path of truth is narrow, but a hair can be a bridge for an ant. We must be like ants, very small, humble, with no self-importance if we are to understand the subtlety of the path of truth. Once we do this, we fall into the awe and majesty of our Creator. He beckons us towards Him.

Our true self is our soul, and the soul is connected to our Creator. When we learn to satisfy our soul instead of satisfying our worldly desires we become truly satisfied. When the veils have been lifted from our soul we reside in reality, and we are connected to the Eternal as opposed to the temporary.

If we can get to the point where forgiveness is part of our essence, where love is part of our essence, where handling situations appropriately is part of our essence, then everyone we come in contact with shares in that essence. In that sharing, those around us begin to come to an elevated state.

Intend to enter into a stream of consciousness with God. Talk directly and spontaneously to God. Enter into a place where we speak without speaking. Speak without preconception, from a place where we stay in the moment, where we are not aware of the past or the future. If we allow anxiety in, the words will stop. We need to learn how to speak to God freely.

The gratification of our senses is not the purpose of our existence, our purpose is to know who we really are. We are not this being of flesh and bone, we are a being of light. Until we understand this light being we do not know the truth about ourselves, we have limited ourselves to the knowledge of the senses. We exist beyond our senses. The universe, all that exists and all that can be, exists within us.

Opposites do not coexist, something to remember when we find ourselves in the state of love's opposites, when we are hasty, when we are angry, resentful, or jealous. Even though we might feel justified it makes no difference, we are the vessel for these. Since we ourselves are the vessel containing the resentment, it means the acid of resentment corrodes us. Since we ourselves are that vessel containing the anger, it means the acid of anger is burning us.

There are consequences to love. There are consequences to forgiveness. There are consequences to compassion and mercy. These consequences open a door within us to further our understanding of love, forgiveness, compassion, and mercy. They open our hearts to be able to imbibe the qualities of God in greater and greater amounts.

Love invites the lovers of God. Jealousy invites the jealous. As we become lovers of God, we become more loveable, more lovely. As we become more lovely we are easier to be with and we are easier to love. If we want to be loved become lovable, become lovely. It is not about other people becoming more lovely for us, it is about us becoming more lovely for them.

Some of us define ourselves by the praise and blame of the world. If the world praises us we define ourselves as great, and when the world blames us we define ourselves as something other than great. We need to become integrated enough within ourselves, and integrated enough with understanding who we are, that we are not affected by the praise and blame of those around us.

Our mind does not live in this moment, it lives in the future or in the past. The future and the past both have the same reality in our mind. Once we engage the future or the past our state is essentially a mental state, not one which involves the heart. Unless we are in a state involving the heart we are not in reality, we are in illusion, we are in the mind which is the ocean of illusion.

We need to become healed. We need to be our own doctor. No one else is going to heal us. We need to become physically healed and psychologically healed. We need to become healed in the most profound way possible which is to become pure, free of elemental influences. In that purity we can reside in a state of love. Then the world has no impact on us.

❧

Pettiness and dignity cannot abide with each other. Dignity has an overriding sense of forgiveness, of calming things down, as opposed to making small things into larger things. Dignity hides the faults of others. Dignity has a way of bringing peace to situations as opposed to inciting situations. Dignity does not have jealousy. Dignity does not have envy. Dignity is an overriding maturity that takes into account the difficulties and foibles of others and soothes them.

❧

We need to develop our witness, the conscience, which watches and knows what is appropriate in our lives, and knows what is not appropriate. It must be steady and consistent. God will support this effort. For every step we take towards Him, He takes ten steps towards us.

It is very easy to talk about love. It is very easy to talk about compassion. It is very easy to talk about forgiveness. It is very difficult to bring them into actuation, to bring them into reality. In order to truly understand forgiveness we need to be able to live forgiveness, we need to go through the act of forgiving. Living forgiveness is an entirely different paradigm of existence. This is why it is said that Sufism is not a philosophy, it is a way of being.

According to the prophets our true state is one of great illumination. Each human being is a light shining through millions of universes. This world is just a tiny atom, but appearances make it seem much larger. The light within each of us is greater than we imagine, greater than our vision, greater than anything we can see, hear, taste, smell, or touch, it is beyond our comprehension. God has placed this light in us, a light whose strength we need to understand but not take pride in. Bow to it, be obedient to it, be humble before it. That is our higher state, the state we need to develop inwardly, become worthy vessels to carry God's light in God's way.

Our inner witness is our conscience, our inner teacher. If the witness is sufficiently developed, if we keep out of its way, we see that the witness knows right from wrong. When our witness is developed in knowledge and wisdom, when understanding how to act correctly is on automatic, it is no longer attached to the world, it is attached to God. We need to reach that point where we follow our conscience at all times.

The inner turmoil we experience when we attempt to change our circumstances makes it impossible for us to be peaceful. When we are in a state of turmoil, emotional elemental disturbances erupt inside us, which make us react. We think we are supposed to alter our external circumstances to find peace. We think peace is found by adjusting our circumstances to suit our definition of peace. Instead, search for the peace that is not connected to the elemental world.

In prayer we alter the nature of our interaction with the world, we withdraw from the conflicts of life by focusing on a higher Being, surrendering to the higher Being, surrendering to His trust and care. By surrendering, we are connected to the underlying perfection of everything, matching our vibration to God's vibration. Then we can find peace.

We each have a spigot which releases the pure rain of God to wash away the dramas, dilemmas, and problems in our lives. This spigot releases the wisdom and purity which resolves our difficulties. Accessing this spigot depends on knowing how to get out of the way, a process which entails deep faith, and the disappearance of selfhood. When that happens there is unlimited guidance available to us. We need to have faith that the ability to achieve this exists within us, that there is a Creator who is deeply in touch with us, guiding us, and giving us what we need.

If we want to know the truth, we need to find a way to involve ourselves with the truth. On the Sufi path we do not have to go anywhere to participate in it, it is all here. It is all within us. All we need to do is put ourselves in a situation where we can contemplate. That contemplation can be called mediation. It can be called prayer.

Strong faith is a key to ridding ourselves of fears, strong faith is a key to shattering the rock which has surrounded our hearts. We need to understand truth, softness, and the melting heart which is the heart of a lover of God. We must have the courage to be unafraid.

When we pray we need to declare our intention, set our intention to have something happen inwardly. When we pray we need to form the intention to make our connection to God. If we reach a state of peace our base desires are quiet, if they are quiet we can be in touch with our undifferentiated soul, connected to God's peace.

✿

The steps taking us to wisdom are steps of appropriate inner thought and appropriate outer action. Without that combination we cannot move forward. If our thoughts are filled with desire how can we move to a higher consciousness? If our thoughts are filled with greed how can we move to a higher consciousness? If our thoughts are filled with jealousy how can we move to a higher consciousness? If we have thoughts of resentment or hate how can we move to a higher consciousness? A higher consciousness cannot coexist with these qualities.

✿

We need to be in a loving state, find ways to be in loving situations, be among those who offer love and kindness. We need to care for others and forget about ourselves. As we forget about ourselves our attention can be focused somewhere else, where the opportunity to love exists.

There needs to be a real connection between ourselves and others. That connection truly occurs when our hearts feel the pain of those around us, when our hearts feel the happiness of those around us, when our hearts feel the state of those around us, and feels God in those around us.

⁂

Truth is hidden within us. If our attention is focused on the world then our interest in God, our awareness of God, our yearning for God may wane. We have a choice, we can either take hold of the world and consume it, or rid ourselves of these desires, change our focus, and change our attention.

⁂

We need to understand our place in existence. This is what enlightened beings have been teaching–reality, not the business of the world. We are a function of God's supreme grace independent of nation, religion, or race. When we recognize that the entire universe exists in one's heart, we no longer embrace the world's definition of who we are which denies our true state. We exist at the center, not as a soul apart. Become centered in the boundless glory of God's own might, and then strive to fulfill His request to become enlightened.

Just like any other ocean, the ocean of illusion becomes still only when we dive very deep, our focus must be deep and powerful. The waves on the surface of the ocean are in constant motion, affected by everything, a passing boat, the winds that blow, storms, but when we go deep below there is a stillness. When we live our lives only on the surface we react to people and situations without thinking. When we go deep within, in touch with the undifferentiated spirit connected to God, we change, we are no longer affected by what happens outside.

If we are so subject to the world that we need its praise, we cannot go on this path. If we free ourselves of the need for that praise, and all that we have accumulated over the years, we can find our way on this path. Then we will understand the treasure, the true way, what really is available. If we have traded our true treasure for a few glittering things that we can touch and see, we have lost our inheritance. We are not what we appear to be, we are not what we see with our eyes, smell with our nose, hear with our ears, we are other than that. Understand our true treasure, concentrate on that because to see with our inner eye takes great concentration, great focus. This is not a small thing, it is the most important thing in our lives.

God is merciful and is going to be merciful towards us. We need to believe in that mercy, we need to believe in that mercy to the degree that we have no fears. Imagine being so confident in God's mercy that we have no fears. If we have no fears, we have no worries.

Someone once defined worry as feeling future pain now, where we have decided that the future is going to be bad. If we think like this, then we have decided what God is going to do. We have decided how God is going to take care of us, and we have decided that He is not going to be merciful towards us.

Understand that our ability to love unconditionally is what saves us, our ability to share this with others is what saves us. It needs to be emphasized and understood that our ability to love brings us closer to the Great Love. Our ability to have compassion brings us closer to the Great Compassion. Our ability to be merciful brings us closer to the Great Mercy. We are the qualities that we exist in. If we cannot become the qualities of love, compassion, and mercy, we separate ourselves from everyone else.

We cannot be full of the world and expect simultaneously to be full of God. We need to choose one or the other. We are told that we are given free will and we are. We have one choice to make. Choose the world or choose God. Everything flows from that choice. Every decision we make in our lives is a function of that choice.

When love enters the equation, when we learn to love for the sake of love and not for the sake of anything else, when we learn to love for the sake of the truth in each of us, for God's sake, for the sake of the great holy beings and the prophets, everything inside us begins to change, our hearts begin to melt.

Once we get into the state of correct action we can get into the state of correct being. Once that combination of action and being are alive in us in a profoundly correct way then we are at the doorstep of reality, we are at the doorstep of knowing the truth, we are at the doorstep of the treasures of grace being opened to us and being shown to us. These treasures are greater than anything we can imagine.

When we are immature we do many things without thought or understanding. Part of being immature is being reactive as opposed to having purpose. Part of being immature is reacting in the moment as opposed to considering consequences. Part of being immature is immediate gratification of the senses as opposed to contemplating the consequences of that gratification.

In prayer, we alter the nature of our interaction with the world, we withdraw from the conflicts of life by focusing on God, surrendering to God, trusting in Him. The ability to release ourselves from interacting with external things, leaving all that in God's hands, changes our elemental nature. By surrendering, we are connected to the underlying perfection of everything, matching our vibration to the vibration of God, then we are at peace.

For those of us who want to go on the path of understanding the unseen, we need to give up what is seen. We need to give up our attachments to everything we can touch. We need to give up our attachments to everything we collect. We need to give up our attachments to everything that separates us from others.

71

When we set forth an intention to align ourselves with qualities that are holy, when we intend to align ourselves with the qualities that are God's, we then begin to merge with those qualities. If we intend and yearn for this, then these qualities can be revealed to us. After we establish a personal intention, aligning ourselves with these qualities, we begin to see the merging of God's qualities in every aspect of our lives.

We are unaware of the scars in our consciousness that greed creates, unaware of the scars in our consciousness that resentment creates, we are unaware of the damage that ill will creates. We think ill will towards others punishes them, but the container holds the acid. The container of our being is damaged by the acids of jealousy, resentment, anger, and hatred. These are the acids that destroy our very being.

To change our destiny we need to climb the rungs of consciousness. We need to escape from the animal intellect into discernment. We need to climb from discernment to wisdom, and begin to understand the reality of existence. As we come closer to this reality, wisdom begins to burn away the darkness of our existence.

We have an inner witness who truthfully examines our actions, a witness with knowledge, with the wisdom to know the difference between right and wrong. When that witness sees an inappropriate action it says, "Stop, I see what you are doing," and we must respond in an appropriate way. That witness is our conscience, our inner teacher. If we do not block the inner witness, non-elemental love which knows right from wrong comes forth. When we turn to our inner witness, we understand through wisdom how to act appropriately.

Subatomic particles do not react in the same way that atomic particles react in the world. If we use Newtonian physics for subatomic particles we do not get the results we think we will.

Spirituality is like this, understanding reality is like this. Once we understand that within what we see there are layers of things going on which we do not see. These layers are the building blocks of what we do see. We can understand that there is so much more going on than what we see, there is so much more to experience than what we see. What we see is shorthand for an inability to contemplate reality.

Love and the flow of love are what transform us. The blockage of love is what degrades us. We need to understand that if a religion puts conditions on love, then there is something wrong with the way that religion is being preached, and it has lost its connection to truth.

❦

There is a very interesting phenomenon that happens to many of us, we can get to the point where we fall in love with our ideas, where we believe there is truth in our ideas. When our ideas are not based in the truth we become hypnotized by them. We need to be aware of these attachments to illusion.

❦

When we truly believe that bringing love to the world will change it, we need to be prepared to do that, to love. We need to accept the responsibility to share what we have had the grace to receive and let it pass through us and spread to everyone else. Walk love around, hand it out, love is not something to keep for ourselves. If we try to hold onto love it dies, but if we let love pass through us it grows, then we receive so much more than we have ever imagined.

Patience is an umbrella raised over God's throne. As we walk this path we must have patience and faith. We must use certitude and determination as the legs to walk this path or we will turn back. Even though we cannot see the benefits now, we will see the benefits later. The oak tree was once a seed.

❀

We live in a world of praise and blame, a world of opposites where everything has two sides. If we keep searching for the easy way and simultaneously fear the difficult way, we will live in turmoil. As long as we are looking for satisfaction in the world this turmoil goes on, but when we free ourselves of praise and blame the turmoil stops.

❀

Become ready for the extraordinary. Become available to the extraordinary. We need to allow ourselves to be surprised. We need to allow ourselves to be in a place of awe. We need to allow ourselves to be ready for that which will come to us spontaneously that will show us the truth.

If we treat people according to their lowest functioning state, they will respond from that state. Invoking the lowest potential in others can invoke the same state in ourselves. If we treat people according to their highest state, at the purest truth of their being, their highest potential, they become more elevated and respond from that place.

As long as we cannot endure someone disagreeing with us, how will we sit still long enough to contemplate the truth, contemplate reality? As long as we are so petty that every worldly conflict affects us we do not have time to contemplate the truth. We need to change our nature, change our character, we need to stop being petty.

As we behave with God's qualities over a period of time we develop loyalty to appropriate behavior, loyalty to our fellow beings. Then every action that comes from us, comes through love, with the recognition of God within us all. We do no harm because we understand love, we understand God within us, we have loyalty to God's creations, loyalty to God's way, loyalty to the reason we are here.

We each contain the totality of existence, we are the universe, each one of us. In order for the universe to pour out patience we need to be the ones pouring out patience, in order for the universe to pour out generosity we need to be the ones pouring out generosity, in order for the universe to pour out love we need to be the ones pouring out love. Otherwise, we interfere with the natural flow of things.

What tells us we are in the midst of an extraordinary moment, an extraordinary experience? We know when we watch an appropriate intention come to fruition. If we intend to be filled with flowing love and we see that happen, if we feel this love which is part of us spread to others, we are changed, altered, we have learned not to measure with our mind. This is an extraordinary moment.

When we interact with others does our state bring love to the equation, are we a soothing balm to the wounds of the world, or are we like salt? Are we sometimes that balm and sometimes salt? Do we recognize when we act like salt, do we recognize when we are a healing balm? Do we focus purposefully on what we do, can we make love our essence?

There are some seedlings in a forest which need a fire to germinate, to produce new life. And so it is with us, we need the fire of love to burn away our base qualities so that truth can grow. There is a thick undergrowth inside of ourselves that must be removed to make room for the light within us to grow. This is the most important part of who we are.

❧

In each of our lives when we move forward towards the truth we need to leave our past. If our past is how we define ourselves, if our past is what we are attached to, if our past is what we are magnetized to and hypnotized by, we cannot live in the moment, we live in illusion because the past no longer exists.

We also need to let go of the future, let go of our ideas of what is going to happen next, of how we are going to accomplish something, of what we need to do, of what we need to have before we can begin whatever it is that we want to start. We have these impediments from the past, and we have barricades from our thoughts of the future. We are pulled into the past by our attachment to it, and we are pulled into the future by our imagination of it.

Attachments to the world make it difficult to stay in a state of love, we keep finding external conditions which we think need to be changed. The process of changing outer circumstances pulls us away from love. We rationalize this and insist that things have to be a certain way, we continuously rearrange everything that bothers us, putting all our focus and intention on outer attachments.

It is only when we pull ourselves off the canvas of illusion, and step outside of time, and be content in that space, that we begin to enter reality. This is an important understanding.

With this understanding we can dramatically change our nature, our attitudes, our way, and our lives. In those moments when we leave the canvas of illusion, truth will come to us. The words that flow through us will become our own teacher. The words that flow through us will show us the way. We need to understand how that works, and how to become involved in that.

We are not our language, we are not our color, we are not our religion, we are not the ideas that we grew up with, we are not our parents, we are not any of these things. There is something else, something that we cannot see, something that we cannot touch, something that we cannot feel that is really what is keeping us alive. In the same way that we cannot see the air that we breathe but need it to stay in existence, we cannot see this Power that maintains us, but it keeps us in existence. Strive to become more aware of this Power.

On the Sufi path we find peace and freedom. The obsessions of the world produce many difficulties in our lives; there is only one obsession with a cure, the obsession to know God. This is what we must engage, this is the obsession to practice, a practice called prayer, called the remembrance of God. Focus on God's qualities of love, compassion, tolerance, peacefulness, focus on acquiring these qualities. Let us look at the qualities we have and realize their implications. Are we merciful or hateful, aloof or loving, jealous or content, grateful or lost in desire? Mercy, contentment, and gratitude do not depend on what we have on the outside, they depend on who we are inside.

A truly great saint can bring peace to a large area because of the resonance which accompanies him or her, a resonance aligned with truth. If we develop this we can bring peace to those we know, those we spend time with, we can change lives without words, just by being who we are.

With that true stillness we change, we can feel a vibration within ourselves. We experience the silent transforming vibration as it travels through different parts of our body, it is real, this resonance exists. Not only do we feel this vibration, but those who are close to us can also feel the vibration. This resonance can change our world. We need to let this happen by staying in that state of balance, having no reaction when the world invites us to react.

We need to understand and learn the nature of the mind. Once we understand how it works, we need to disengage from it. If we are engaged with the mind, listening to it and doing what it says, wherever it goes we are going to follow. Freedom happens when we disengage from the mind. This is where we become discerning, disengaged from our desire-based needs. Once this has awakened within us we find our own freedom. Then there is a chance for our ascendance into transcendence.

Free will comes down to a simple choice we make, do we believe there is a Supreme Power governing all that exists or do we deny this? If we believe in a Supreme Power governing everything, do we attempt to align ourselves with that Supreme Power or not? This is the extent and range of our free will. What are the consequences for us? The Supreme Power flows and we decide whether we are going to move with the flow or fight against it. Deciding to flow with the Supreme Power is a major step towards aligning ourselves with it, quite an adventure. The consequence of not choosing to be in the flow is being excluded from the grace of reality. This is the choice we have been given, this is our free will.

We are what we carry around. We are our qualities. If we walk around with resentment, whether we think it is righteous or not, it is still resentment. If someone has wronged us deeply and we have resentment, it is still resentment. Righteous anger is still anger. As long as we believe there can be appropriate anger, appropriate resentment, appropriate jealousy, or an appropriate version of any inappropriate quality, we create an inappropriate situation. Anger and resentment can never be justified.

Know that the value and true worth of our lives is not found in what we see with our physical eyes, this worth is not found in what we touch with our hands, not in what we wear on our backs, not in what we display to the world, not in the titles after our names, not in the people we control. Real worth lies somewhere else. Search for this. Our real worth is how much love, compassion, and kindness we walk around with and share with others, and our faith and determination to merge with God. This is our real worth. Strive to achieve this.

The potential to love unconditionally exists within us, and when that love begins to pour out, it is connected to God's cornucopia of love, it is always full, it cannot be emptied. It continues giving because this is the Power which created everything, the Power within everything, above everything, beside every thing, the Power which keeps the universe in place, in existence. If that Power were withdrawn for even a second everything would disappear, but God is merciful.

We were all created with the capacity to live in reality. Even though we have lost our awareness of reality it is revealed in everything we see. Right below the surface of our lives is reality. What happens deep in the ocean cannot be seen at the surface, yet that does not mean it is not there. Reality is close to us, very close.

In fulfilling our responsibility to become a true human being we must understand the roadblocks of the world which try to stop us, understand the obstacles, acquaintances, and experiences that take us off the path. Transcend all of these without harming anyone.

We need to go through the pain of understanding what we have done to others, what we have done to uplift ourselves by putting others down, the power we exercised at the expense of others. When we begin this analysis, begin to know ourselves better and correct ourselves, we come closer to the truth, closer to reality.

To be a vessel of love we need to act with love consistently, or the vessel will corrode when it is opposed. Within ourselves opposing forces are like acid, anger is acid, jealousy is acid, stubbornness is acid, the need for power is acid, all these acids destroy the vessel of love.

What we do outwardly we do inwardly too. If we scream on the outside, inside we are screaming too. If we are outwardly paranoid, we are in constant inner fear. We need to observe our own actions, watch what we do and how we react externally, this is a key to solving our inner problems.

Go to the place of gratitude, understand how much we have been given. Gratitude gives us an understanding of our relationship to the One who gives. Everything we have was given to us, be grateful and understand our obligation to do unto others as He does unto us. In that state we enter the bliss of true understanding, and the state of love and peace.

When we gossip it means no one wants the problem solved, we want the problem to continue because then we can rank each other, we can differentiate higher and lower. We believe the people we gossip about are lower and we are higher—our gratification for arrogance.

God's love is at the heart of everything. We can transform ourselves into love, we can transform ourselves into compassion with His help, His guidance, with His grace, and the help of all the prophets who brought His message. We need to be transformed, become truth itself to enter reality. If we want to know love, we need to act with love. We need to trust in God, have faith, and make a great effort.

When anger comes into our being, it invites all of its friends. The friends of anger are resentment, hatred, and jealousy. Then they begin to have a party inside of us. If we invite love into our being, it also invites its friends. The friends of love are mercy, tolerance, compassion, and forgiveness. Then they have a party. Which party would we rather go to?

When we are unhappy, when we are upset, we need to be powerful enough through prayer, through surrender, through belief systems, to be able to induce a new state in ourselves. We cannot just let ourselves be when we are upset. We cannot follow the mind and indulge in the torpor of hatred, in the torpor of resentment, in the torpor of self-pity. We cannot allow ourselves to do that. That state is not allowing the light in, it is celebrating the darkness within us.

If we have developed an attitude that we cannot succeed, that what we attempt is impossible, what is going to follow is disappointment. Quite simply, positivity breeds positivity, negativity breeds negativity.

We need to understand this truth, and believe this deep in ourselves, deep in our hearts, deep in our thoughts.

If we cannot be positive, we should at least act positively, because in acting, we surround ourselves with the thoughts of the possibility of the positive. We need to constantly bring the positive to the forefront, and as this is done, we develop an entirely new way of thinking.

We veil ourselves with specific thought patterns, with the way we perceive ourselves to be. We are blinded in our relationships with women, with men, with money, to age, to pain, to sickness, to health, blinded to thousands of things. As long as we are not thinking of our relationship to God we are stuck in torpor. When we consider our relationship to God we climb up the ladder, we climb out from the holes we put ourselves into. When our relationship to God increases, thinking about ourselves in an egocentric way decreases.

On the Sufi path we have an infinite number of thresholds to cross. Each one beckons us to call it home, yet if we decide to stay at any one of them we stop being a pilgrim and become a defender of thresholds. This means that every time we have reached a new plateau, every time we catch a glimpse of grace and say, "I've got it now," we have stopped progressing. We need to have the steadfast humility which reminds us that the road is long, the journey continues, there is no time to stop and we must keep going.

We need to examine our motives in every situation. If we do not examine ourselves through our inner witness, our conscience, we are susceptible to everything around us. We need to learn how to turn away from everything where our motives are self-serving. The only thought which will make us turn away is the understanding that there is a reward, a great treasure, something of immense worth, waiting for us, well beyond what the world has to offer. We find this treasure by being immersed in the qualities of God instead of the qualities of the world.

When we are at the point where we are at the service of others, and we give freely to others, with a smile and with true intention, then we have changed. We need to reside in this place, then the joy we find there becomes the joy in our lives. This joy becomes the grace in our lives. The blessings of this state become the blessings in our lives. The protection of this place becomes the protection in our lives. Then our lives become one of a true human being.

Let us each form the intention that our lives will be like this. Let us each form the intention that this will be the way we go. Let us each form the intention that this is the path we take to fulfill our birthright.

About the Author

Musa Muhaiyaddeen (Emanuel L. Levin) grew up in New Jersey with his mother, father and brother. He attended law school at Boston University, and practiced law in New Jersey for many years. He is also entrepreneurial and has created various businesses. Musa is a devoted husband, father of three, and grandfather of six

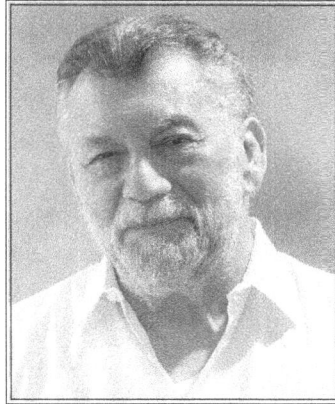

When Musa was in his twenties, he and his wife met the Sufi teacher, M. R. Bawa Muhaiyaddeen in Philadelphia. They quickly recognized Bawa's enormous wisdom, kindness, and love, and became his disciples. Musa and his family moved to Philadelphia to be near Bawa and learn from him. Shortly after meeting Bawa, Musa was told by Bawa to teach others what he had been learning. This began Musa's journey of sharing his wisdom and insights, and inspiring others on the Sufi Path towards God.

Musa has a rare gift for making the teachings of Sufism accessible to Westerners. He teaches in a very grounded way, distilling esoteric concepts into useable and understandable language. Musa explains that Sufism goes beyond all languages, religions, and cultural backgrounds. This is a path open to all seekers of the unseen, those striving to connect to their inner spiritual life, to give them new meaning and direction.

To quote Musa, "There is this mystery of man's relationship to God. Every person has this relationship. We need to explore this relationship and make that exploration something that is a life-long priority. We identify with our body, but we are not our body. Similarly, we identify with our culture, language, and religion, but we are not any of those things either. Our true story is the story of our real identity. We need to find what and who that is. Just as we have duties to our family and within the work-sphere, at the same time we also need to do what is necessary to understand where reality is, and who we are in that reality. That, in fact, is our primary duty."

The quotes in this book are taken from the spontaneous weekly talks Musa gives in Philadelphia. You can hear hundreds of Musa's discourses on his website, www.thewitnesswithin.com. Musa Muhaiyaddeen's books are available on Amazon.

Other books by Musa Muhaiyaddeen
Available on Amazon

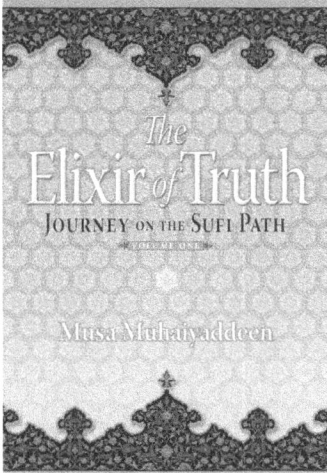

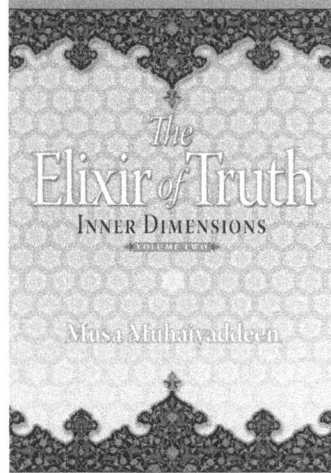

The Elixir of Truth:
Journey on the Sufi Path, *Volume 1*

and

The Elixir of Truth:
Inner Dimensions, *Volume 2*

Musa's books are also available in Kindle and epub ebook formats.

Essays, audio, and video discourses in English
are available for free at
www.thewitnesswithin.com